Boy From The Poems

VISVESHWAR

INDIA · SINGAPORE · MALAYSIA

Copyright © Visveshwar 2023
All Rights Reserved.

This book has been published with all efforts taken to make the material error-free after the consent of the author. However, the author and the publisher do not assume and hereby disclaim any liability to any party for any loss, damage, or disruption caused by errors or omissions, whether such errors or omissions result from negligence, accident, or any other cause.

While every effort has been made to avoid any mistake or omission, this publication is being sold on the condition and understanding that neither the author nor the publishers or printers would be liable in any manner to any person by reason of any mistake or omission in this publication or for any action taken or omitted to be taken or advice rendered or accepted on the basis of this work. For any defect in printing or binding the publishers will be liable only to replace the defective copy by another copy of this work then available.

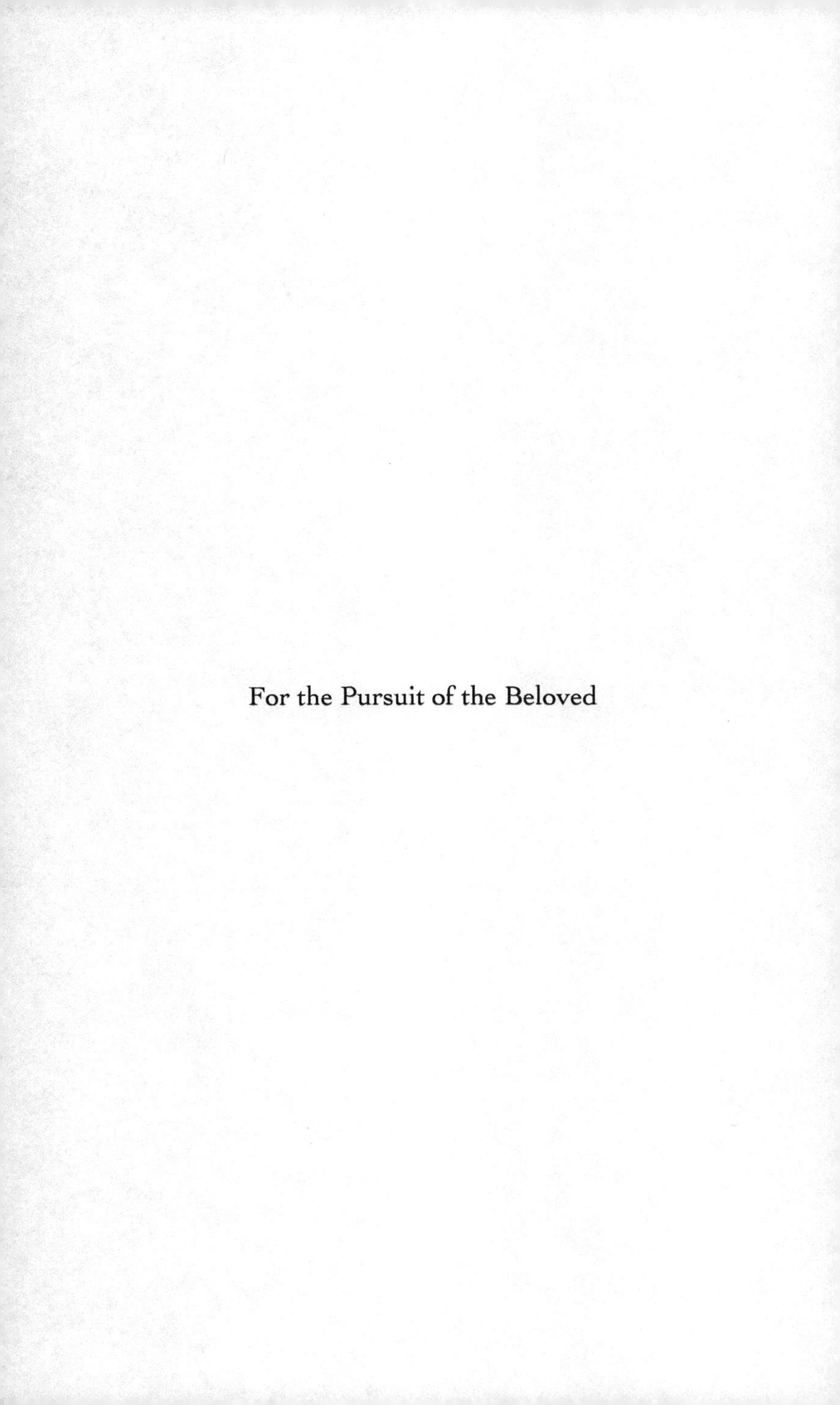

For the Pursuit of the Beloved

Contents

Foreword: Love & Its Object

We confuse love with the object of love. Love is not the same as the lover or the beloved. The beloved is only the carrier of love. It is love which makes the beloved important, not the other way around. But we normally lack this clarity. This results in mistaking the person to be more important than love itself and this leads to conflict.

That is not to say that persons are not important. Without persons there is no way love can be experienced. When the lover identifies with the beloved, then the beloved becomes more important, and love becomes the casualty. Only when love and the vehicles of love—the lover and the beloved—are in sync, can love be experienced as the movement of creative joy. Love, then, can include the whole Universe. In its essence, love is the connection between the individual self and the Self of the Universe. The beloved can then be seen as the symbol or the representation of the Self.

In these poems, Visveshwar has explored the various shades and nuances of love with great sensitivity and sensibility. In his eyes, the beloved never fully becomes concretised. The beloved is elusive, hard to catch and

hold in words or images. Every line, every moment,
is a promise, but cannot be captured and held, and
slips into the next moment, the next line.

The elusive beloved thus becomes even
more precious and valuable. The incapacity and
limitedness of the concrete mind are brought to
light in his skillful use of language. Images that flow
in harmony convey directly to the reader's heart the
pain of separation, the pining for the beloved, and
the longing for union. A quiet, nearly unheard voice
seems to speak the poems, elevating the reading of
these verses to a subtle and heightened experience.

As one reads these poems, one feels the clear
presence of the beloved in one's own heart, as a
sweet pain that takes us into unknown depths.

I look forward to more poems from Visveshwar,
deepening the journey of love, the search for and
the discovery of the beloved.

Anandh Krishna

21 July 2022

*Anandh is the author of 13 books of fiction, essays and
poetry in Tamil. His first book in English is forthcoming.*

Preface

Each piece of writing in this collection offers a unique glimpse of moments experienced in my inner world. I wanted to keep them, rather like photographs from a land far away.

And what does it mean to me to share them with the world? First, there is the rush of excitement to be "out there", visible and tangible. And second, I find immense joy in sharing artistic expressions.

Thank you for joining me on this journey.

Visveshwar

July 2022

BITTERSWEET

Summer Breeze

All it takes is a skein of summer breeze

to teleport me…

To the summer

when I was little,

eating mango icecream with my cousins

after we played in the kids swimming pool.

To the summer
when I was walking
in the school garden after class,
listening to a carol,
wishing to be a part of it.

To the summer
when I was on the college bus,
warmed by the July sun,
looking outside the window,
listening to the same song on loop,
with my head sunken in the blues.

Then to those summers
that I don't want to remember...
those summers that I skip
like I'm skipping on a hot floor.

I wonder what it'll take to teleport me
to those summers that I will spend with him...

Unknown Saviour

Intoxicated by a teenage dream, I walk through workspaces, still smelling of cream biscuits, wanting to be saved but don't know from what.

Ms. Daisy had no idea that in my past life I used to be that girl from the palace who died a tragic death and reincarnated as the little boy in front of her. Maybe that's why I was tired! Isn't it tiring to rise from the dead?

Middle school was about wearing white trousers on Wednesdays, falling for tall senior boys while they chased girls with coloured hair. I was so out of place, I still am.

Evenings were by default dulled by a mild sorrow and the fears of what the next day would bring. Everyone wanted me to go to school while I kept waiting for Sundays. Like an ink blot, sorrow soaked through each whole day, then drenched the entire calendar too. Then came the times where there was no point in waiting for weekends or vacations. There was nothing to wait for.

And now I'm here, feeling homesick at home, waiting to be saved by "him" whom I don't know and from something that no one knows, including me, and to promise me I'm safe, that I can let my guard down and sleep and that he'll be here when I wake up and I don't have to wait anymore…

Cherry Soda

Sipping cherry soda on a winter night, I match my footsteps with his, on an unknown street. A drowsy moon floats somewhere in a purple sky with calm stars. I wonder if the world can hear anything but our footsteps together and my home keys in his pocket.

It's 2 a.m., even the street lights are sleepy. But I don't care, for I can sleep when I get home, when I get home with him. Closed shop shutters shiver in the cold; I shiver too, for he is a foot apart.

I whisper his name into his ear, but he walks as if
he doesn't hear. I chatter my teeth louder for him to
notice. He smiles yet acts as if he doesn't care. I call
out his name, waking his senses and a few birds too.

He pulls me close and kisses me to silence. My teeth
stop their chatter, night blushes into dawn. I inhale
his warmth and snuggle into his chest. His stubble
tickles my neck and I wake from sleep...

Sipping rosemary tea on my white bed, I watch
the sky outside the window, wondering when the
purple turned pink, who he is and what his name
is...

Wake Up With Me

I don't want to sleep with him.
But I want to wake up with him,
for my wings get bruised in the mornings
as I fall from the world of dreams
to the world of decisions and deadlines.

I want him to hold me in his big arms
as I wake, and to whisper in my ear
that I can always go back to him
after a day on earth or even after
the morning walk or even after
striking one item off my to-do list,
or I don't have to leave him at all.

Come Find Me

Sometimes I mistake others for you,
for I see your eyes in someone,
hear your voice from someone,
feel your touch in someone.

I give away parts of myself
hoping you are one of them.
I return empty-hearted for
none of them is you.

Now I let go of everyone that's not you
to make space for everything that's you.
Your eyes, your smile, your warmth too,
your voice, your scent, your love that's due.

I keep losing myself in search of you,
floating through days and nights
needing everything that's you and
missing everything that's you…

Come find me before I vanish.

Souvenir

What choice do I have dear boy?
For, I'm now mere a heart
with arms that held you and
legs that walked with you...

What made you play the piano that night
when I was alone under the moonlight?
What made me sing to you that song
that I hid most of my love in?

What made you ask me out for a night walk
and what made me say yes?
What made you ask me if you can hug me
and what made me nod yes?

What made us kiss, and bask in each other's
warmth in your messy room?
What made you drop me back home
after we hit the heights of heavens?

What choice do I have dear boy?
I remember everything but all I'm left with now
is the sweet pain as the souvenir
from the world I chose to visit with you...

SWEET NOTHINGS

Something about Him

There's something about him. He has those vintage vibes. He is young yet it feels as if he has always been around and has seen years that he has never lived. He smells sweet like vanilla and sometimes warm like cinnamon.

We exchange sweet nothings in the evening, lying together on the oranges in the back of his truck, parked under a maple tree. He points to something in the wine-stained sky. I'd rather look at his beautiful arm and his fingers…

He stares at me through his sunglasses. "What?" I ask. "Chinku, you shine. I'd like to know how the sun feels when it touches your golden brown skin…" I turn and bury my face in the oranges.

He grabs me by my waist and boom, I wake up from my dream. It's afternoon and I'm on my bed. Cinnamon and cloves in butter signal lunch being cooked. Song plays on the radio: *Don't cry about him, don't cry about him, it's all gonna happen…*

Lavender

The lavender in the seal of the envelope has started to wither. I almost forgot what I wrote for you. It was a Wednesday and my room was lit bright by the afternoon sun and I didn't care to go back to work. I was wearing a faded green linen shirt, not fully buttoned, sleeves rolled up a bit and loose beige pants. I was sipping rose tea and some dream pop was playing. I wanted you, or at least your voice near me.

I can go on and on about how much I remember. They say that I remember way too much. But only I know how much I have forgotten. Remind me of everything that I need to be reminded of. Remind me of myself, remind me of the sound of my laughter. Bring to me that which I don't know I need but actually do. Take me to times where everything is exciting and I don't want to sleep at all. Yet I sleep because you are with me.

I still wait, wait for your footsteps near my doorstep. I wait for the roars of your bike to echo all over my unswept parking space.

I'll water my plants and feed the fish tomorrow but how do I post this letter when I don't know where you live and don't know who you are?

Flame of the Forest

I put you in a song and myself too. We stand under a flame of the forest near the stadium of the school ground. You stand tall before me. The shape of your face, your wristwatch and the fact that tomorrow is Sunday, all feel so good together, like the pink and orange evening sky. Don't ask me why, because you know me.

Summer is warm enough but I still hug you from
behind while we ride through the narrow city
streets. We don't count calories while we munch
on the street treats and I don't have to count the
minutes we spend together because I know it is
forever, our bike rides, the songs that you sing for
me over phone every night…

Tomorrow we'll meet in the school ground. The
colour of the sky might be different but I know all
the colours of your love. I know that you know
how exciting it is for me when you come to me
every evening, to the school ground and how much
I cherish the certainty you bring by just showing
up. Doesn't matter if you are smiling or tired,
I always have space for your tenderness on my
shoulders.

Hey Boy

Hey boy, be my cake
and I'll be your jam.
Let's jam on my balcony,
or dance to your favourites.
Play me like your guitar,
but play no games,
no games.

Hey boy, it's okay
to kiss me if you want to.
No one will know but
you, me and my table plant.
Come to bed, let's
have some cookies.
I won't complain if you
drop some crumbs.

Hey boy, don't rush,
the clock is frozen
and so is everything.
Forget traffic, forget work,
you're that boy from the poems
and I'm your one true love,
we are the last two flames of fire
coming together to burn
everything but love.

Night's Blue

It's time for him to leave. I'm on my balcony, letting his fingers go one by one from my hand as he descends the secret stairs...

Dancing shadows of sleeping trees fill the street, stars shimmer amidst sugar woven clouds. The night's blue stains the city. A cold breeze shivers over my body, I miss him.

I wrap my palms around the floral handrail and strain to glimpse him. He returns my glance with a half crescent smile, his eyes moonlight tender. He waves, mounts his bike and rides away like art… He is art just by being and I'm his admirer.

I walk back towards the door as the roars of his bike fade into the night's calm. Tomorrow he will come, then all our tomorrows, too.

Meditate on Me

Meditate on me
over the terrace lawn.
Look at me like you look at
gardens, oceans and heavens.
Play for me melodies
from worlds you've been to.

Touch me before I disappear,
explore me like new music.
Put your ear on my heart,
tell me I'm alive.

Dance with me on the lane
where dreams meet reality.
Pull me, push me, but
don't drop me. Let's dance
till we get dizzy and
fall out of time, but
let's fall together.

Trace my veins,
listen to my blood flowing.
Visit all my edges, curves,
slopes and corners.
Switch all the lights off,
let me keep finding myself
every time you meditate on me.

SWEET ESCAPE

Never Let Me Go

I wake up to my alarm, pick up my favourite clothes from the pile on the floor which I don't have to fold anymore. From the mess of my dim-lit, cramped room, I take my card, his love letters, and the little cash that's left and stuff everything into my backpack. I grab the car keys and slip my feet into my old canvas shoes. I leave the door open, it doesn't matter anymore...

I run upstairs, push the half open door, kiss and wake him. He sits up and rests his head on my chest. I bury my face into his messy hair and wrap my arms around him. He smells like chocolate and peppermint and everything I need. My heart races. I cup his face and whisper, "It is late…"

He kisses me back, tumbles out of bed, slips into his denims, looks at the mirror, and tousles his hair. He winks at me watching him. I jump up, hug him from behind, raise my heels to rest my chin on his shoulder, and glimpse us in the mirror.

I button his shirt up, his bag is packed. He puts on rugged running shoes, wraps me in his pullover to keep me warm. He leaves the door open, it doesn't matter anymore…

We get into the car and drive—away from noise, opinions, hatred and hurt. The radio plays, *Drive me in your car until the sky gets big, never let me go…*

Prince

It is evening and I walk with him,
around the water garden at his palace.
The swans stop swimming and watch.
His white, long sleeved shirt
feels like breeze on me; I love
how I don't have to ask
to borrow his clothes anymore.

I hear distant sounds of bells,
calls of peahens and peacocks.
A sublime scent of
spices wafts about us.

The warmth that I feel
from his palm in mine
keeps me safe from
winter winds, from the
wicked world.

I wrap my arms around his,
lay my head on his shoulder…
I rest, I rest, I rest.

Under the Lemon Tree

I feel home when I'm in his arms.
He is my happy place, a tree's shade
after a hundred years of summer.
I'm all the music that echoes in his home
and all his terrace plants
that smile at him every morning.

I'm not his secret, he shows me off.
He is not afraid to hold my hand
when everyone is watching.
We play footsie under the lemon tree
by the stream, while
the whole world knocks
on closed doors,
looking for us.

I care about nothing,
for I am safe on his shoulder,
listening to his heartbeats
and his sweet breaths…

For Us

I was lost
under what they said about me.
I wore all their words,
weighing more than my bones,
carrying them everywhere I went.

I couldn't find myself
beneath those dirty fingerprints.
It was not me I saw
in the mirror, but I found
myself for you, for me, for us.
I pierced through the sun
to burn it all and to
come to you as I am.

We'll meet under the moon
while the night clouds
float through my hair.
I'll hold your hand
and nothing will weigh me down
while I fly in your love.

Pursuit of the Beloved

The roads that I did not take
held lovers that I did not meet.
Some waited long, some left
and some weren't born at all.

The road I'm taking now
holds that one lover who waits
knowing I'm on the way,
hurrying all I can.

No clock shows the time left,
no milestones on the way either.
Yet wearing my hat, sunscreen
and shoes, I walk. I walk
for myself and for him.

He has planted flowering trees
on my way, asked the birds
to sing when I tire,
and told the cougars
to stay far away.

What else can I do
for myself and for him
but show up on the road
every day?

www.ingramcontent.com/pod-product-compliance
Lightning Source LLC
Chambersburg PA
CBHW031514150726
47990CB00007B/3016